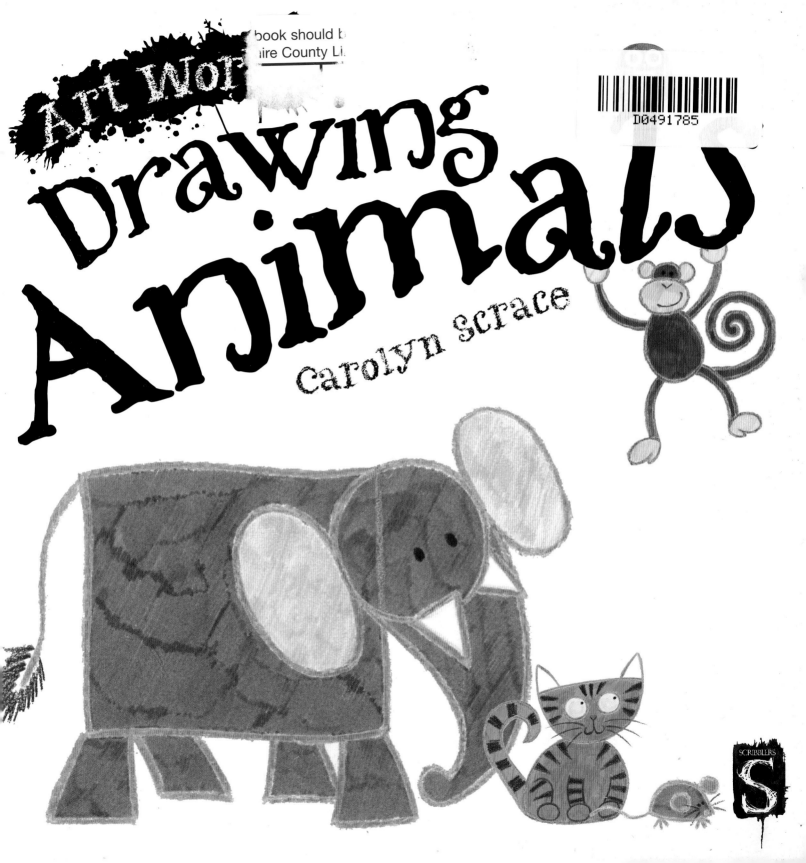

Art Wor

Drawing Animals

Carolyn Scrace

SCRIBBLERS

Author:
Carolyn Scrace graduated from Brighton College of Art, UK, with a focus on design and illustration. Since then she has worked in animation, advertising and children's publishing. She has a special interest in natural history and has written many books on the subject, including *Lion Journal* and *Gorilla Journal* in the *Animal Journal* series.

How to use this book:

Follow the easy, numbered instructions. Simple step-by-step stages enable budding young artists to create their own amazing drawings.

What you will need:

1. Paper to draw on.
2. Wax crayons for drawing.
3. Felt-tip pens to colour in your drawings.

Published in Great Britain in MMXIV by Scribblers, a division of Book House
25 Marlborough Place, Brighton BN1 1UB
www.salariya.com
www.book-house.co.uk

ISBN-13: 978-1-909645-86-8

1 3 5 7 9 8 6 4 2

A CIP catalogue record for this book is available from the British Library.

Printed and bound in China.

PAPER FROM
SUSTAINABLE
FORESTS

Contents

a cat

1 A cat needs a head...

2 ...a body,

3 ...two ears,

4 ...a tail,

5 ...and big, round, green eyes!

6 Now draw his legs and paws.

Finish drawing
in cat's eyes.
Then crayon in
some stripes.

Add a nose,
mouth and
whiskers.

Colour in with
felt-tip pens.

5

 # an owl

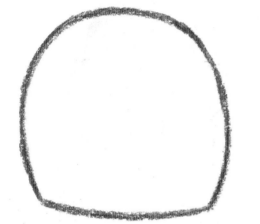

1 An owl needs a body,

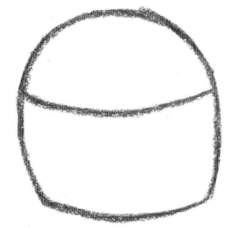

2 ...a head,

3 ...big round eyes,

4 ...two wings,

5 ...a beak and two feet!

6 Now draw in owl's feathers.

Colour in with felt-tip pens.

a zebra

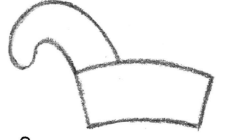

1 A zebra needs a body,

2 ...a neck and head,

3 ...two front legs,

4 ...two back legs,

Mane

5 ...and two ears and a tail!

6 Now crayon in his eyes, nose, mane and the tip of his tail.

8

Add hooves. Draw
in zebra's stripes
using a felt-tip pen.

Hooves

9

a ladybird

1 A ladybird needs a body,

2 ...a head,

3 ...legs,

4 ...an eye,

5 ...and spots!

6 Now colour in her head, spots and legs with felt-tip pens.

Draw in ladybird's
eye and antennae.

Antennae

Colour in with
felt-tip pens.

11

a whale

1 A whale needs a body,

2 ...a tail,

3 ...a flipper,

Blowhole

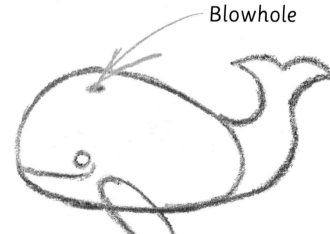

4 ...and an eye, mouth
and blowhole!

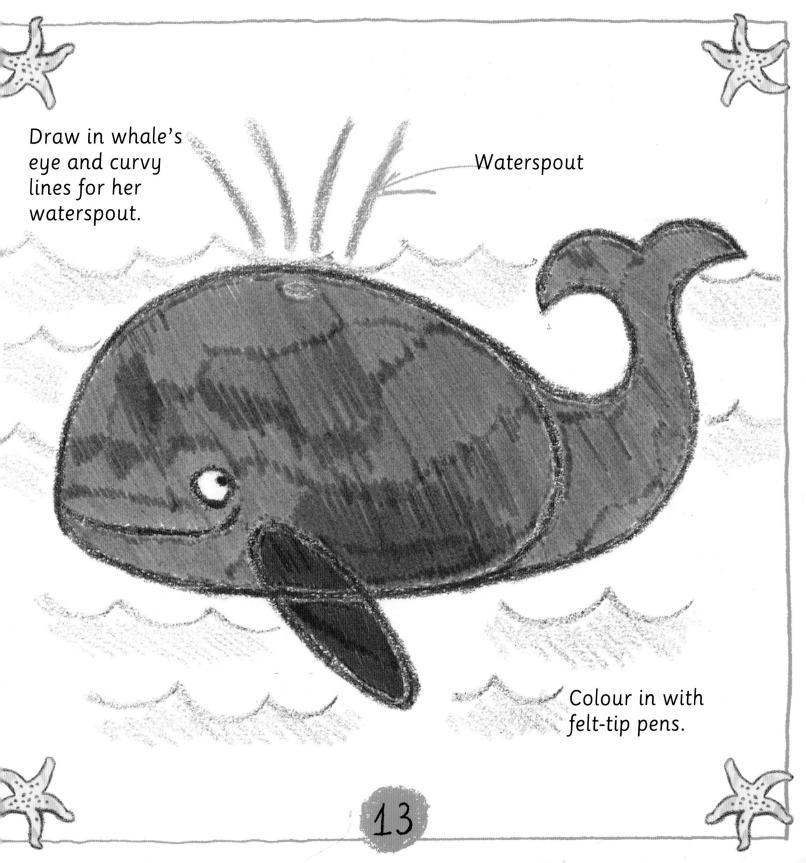

Draw in whale's eye and curvy lines for her waterspout.

Waterspout

Colour in with felt-tip pens.

13

 an elephant

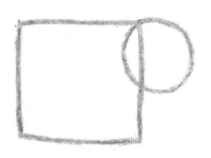

1 An elephant needs a body,

2 ...a head,

3 ...a trunk,

4 ...two big ears,

5 ...four legs,

6 ...and a tail and tusks!

Colour in with
felt-tip pens.

Draw in elephant's
eyes and finish her tail.

15

 # a lion

1 A lion needs a head,

2 ...a body,

3 ...four legs,

4 ...and two ears
and a tail!

Mane

Draw in lion's face and his beautiful big mane.

Colour in with felt-tip pens.

17

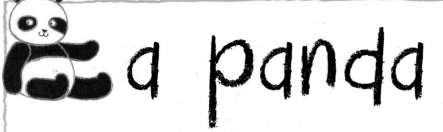 a panda

1 A panda needs a head,

2 ...a body,

3 ...two arms,

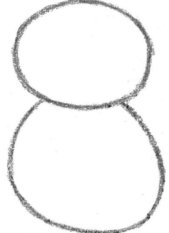

4 ...and two legs!

5 Now draw in panda's markings,

6 ...and his ears and eyes.

Draw in panda's
nose and mouth,
and finish his eyes.

Colour in with
felt-tip pens.

a dog

1 A dog needs a head,

2 ...a body,

3 ...four legs,

4 ...a collar and tail,

5 ...a nose and ears!

6 Crayon in his body.
Leave some white patches.

20

Draw in dog's eyes,
mouth and whiskers.

Add curvy lines to
make him wag
his tail!

Colour in with
felt-tip pens.

21

a frog

1 A frog needs a head,

2 ...a body,

3 ...two legs,

4 ...two feet,

5 ...two arms, two hands,

6 ...great big eyes and spots!

Draw in frog's eyes, nose and mouth.

Colour in with felt-tip pens.

23

a giraffe

1 A giraffe needs a body,

2 ...a long neck,

3 ...four legs,

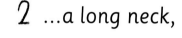

4 ...a head and tail,

5 ...and ears and horns!

6 Draw a square pattern on her neck and body.

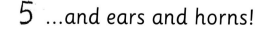

Draw in giraffe's eyes, nose and mouth.

Colour in with felt-tip pens.

25

a fox

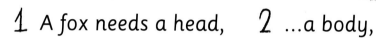

1 A fox needs a head,

2 ...a body,

3 ...a neck,

4 ...four legs,

5 ...a big bushy tail,

6 ...and two ears!
Add an eye.

Draw in fox's nose,
mouth and whiskers,
and finish his eyes.

Draw in his neck,
chest and tail markings.

Colour in with
felt-tip pens.

27

 # a crocodile

1 A crocodile needs a body,

2 ...a tail,

3 ...two eyes and a mouth,

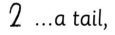

4 ...and four stumpy legs!

5 Now add a zigzag line to the top of crocodile's body.

Draw in his sharp teeth and finish his eyes.

Colour in with felt-tip pens.

a monkey

1 A monkey needs a head,

2 ...a body,

3 ...two arms and two legs,

4 ...two hands and two feet,

5 ...two big ears,

6 ...and a long, curly tail!

Draw in monkey's
eyes, nose and mouth.

Colour in with
felt-tip pens.

31

glossary

Antennae an insect's feelers.

Blowhole what a whale breathes through.

Hooves the hard, lower parts of some animals' feet.

Mane long hair along the neck or round the head of some animals.

Markings different coloured patches on an animal.

Trunk an elephant's nose, used to breathe, suck up water and to pick up food.

Tusk a long, strong pointed tooth, used to get food.

Waterspout spout of water formed when a whale breathes out.

index